In the Folds of Time

Collected Poems

by
Rosy Gallace

Translated into English by
Irma Kurti

In the Folds of Time

Collected Poems

by Rosy Gallace
Translated into English by Irma Kurti

Southern
Arizona
Press

Southern Arizona Press
Sierra Vista, Arizona

In the Folds of Time

By Rosy Gallace
Translated in English by Irma Kurti

First Edition

Author: Rosy Gallace
English Translation: Irma Kurti
Editor: Paul Gilliland
Formatting: Southern Arizona Press
Cover Artwork: Clock - Image by Stones Gucci from Pixabay
Cover Design: Paul Gilliland

Published by Southern Arizona Press
Sierra Vista, Arizona 85635
www.SouthernArizonaPress.com

ISBN: 978-1-960038-37-1

Poetry

Dedication

To all the persons, proud of their own origins…

Preface

I spent most of my childhood years and the better part of my youth basking in the luxuriant nature of my native land on a daily basis.

I was inebriated by the scent of flowers and the taste of fruits and captivated by the bird songs. I communed with nature as I walked along the paths of 'my' forest - an ideal place for meditation, a trusted listener of the little secrets of my heart and that forest served as a sweet balsam to soothe me in my moments of melancholy.

Ever since I moved to the busy, noisy, and frenetic region that is Lombardy, I now often feel a sense of growing nostalgia as I recall those soothing visions, the light of dawn and sunsets, and the clear transparencies of the sky. Today I often feel the vital need for the calmness of that time: to be able to listen to myself, to free my emotions, to draw inspiration from the looks, the gestures and stories of the people I met along the way.

For this reason, in this book of poetry, you will often encounter a lot of nostalgia. You'll also repeatedly read about the words 'light' and 'silence'. Those words express the feelings that truly represent me and those words have accompanied me in many instances (sad or joyful state) of my existence.

ROSY GALLACE

Contents

Sometimes

Sometimes I come to look for you
on rainy evenings,
when the day closes
and the night arrives.

I don't believe in fate.
When you say maybe,
I love only an idea.

I look at the years
that mark the face,
they're the sum of all memories.

Some days I come and look for you
when the heart beats slowly.
In the silence, I hear your steps;
they drift further and further away.

My dream ended like this.
– Imperceptible presence of you –

Dawn arrives and embraces me
the warmth of its light uplifting me.

My hands are leaves on the branches
when the autumn undresses
in front of the bride.

I look at the life that goes by.
A voice reaches me from afar
like a sweet dream
on this growing day.

The "Place of the Heart"

Today,
I came to look for you
in your thoughts,
but I didn't find you.

I passed then by your:
"Place of the heart."
You were in the April wind
among the clothes hanging
on the terrace, in the red silence
of roofs, in the yellow of lemons,
and in the green of the olive trees.

I watched you from behind
the cherry tree, in the passage
of a cloud, while ecstatic you
contemplated the vegetable gardens
in the valley and smelled the still-
green grapes of the vineyard.

I picked up a golden ear
that of me when I'll depart
keep the wonder of a charm
vanished among poppies, wary not to leave
that of my passage still remains
the hidden memory of an ancient summer.

Where Do Memories Go?

I have no more words for you,
only a memory for years to come.
I have no more thoughts to express,
only small stars in the soul carved.

The fiery sunsets on the lake
are nothing more than shaded watercolors
framed on walls against which you hear
mild throbbing inside your chest.

The sound of waves breaking the rocks,
it is only a dirge in the passing hours
along the days stretched out over the years.
I've no more time to tell you about the silences
when the sun blushed the hills.

Evening falls, and the moon appears in the sky
like a coin that could buy the night.
The lukewarm air descends on the city
in the breath of an angel and leafs through
the buildings, as if they were books.

Wrinkles preserve the thoughts
in the evening that everything closes.
The road becomes dark, and the circle
of the sun rolls under the houses.
The sounds chime, the wind dies down,
and I savor the calm that dwells in me now.

Who knows where the memories go…

The sun rises and widens the contours
in my subdued song lost in silence,
sings to me like a lullaby.
The voice in the chest trembles, breathes slowly
like when a life is born, but the memories
come back and hug me again.

Beyond the Words

I think about you a lot these days;
tonight, I gave life to those thoughts.
Maybe you're still sleeping in the blankets
of my memories, maybe because the years
have slipped on us in a flash,
witnesses of time that stopped yesterday.

Images and sounds go beyond words,
piercing like thorns in the throat.
You are like tattoos on the skin
that fade with time, yet are visible lightly,
leaving the meaning intact.

I have looked for you beyond the logic
of whys, beyond any possible answer,
and it is there that I always stumble over
my countercurrent decisions, then run
away in a continuous escape to nothingness.

Everything seems to flow together, yet
time weaves plots in the boundless
winter nights.
You do not answer, and in your silence
explodes my cry of solitude and regrets.

So, I give up.
I give up to voids filled with silences,
to the subtle pain of soul that passes
through invisible threads and pierces
the cold morning air.

It's a sin that you can't hear
my words that go beyond
any logic of what you want
to listen. So you'll never know
how the sun is dressed this morning.

Escape From the City

I remember that summer evening,
the escape from the city, the lakeside restaurant,
the starry sky, the moon, and the boats
like specks in the water.

I remember the music that came
suffused and discreet from the dance halls
and softened the heartbeat.

I remember the white sheets
embroidered like colored plains,
while the yellow light of a lamp
resembled a star that contained dreams.

Dawn came quickly and caught us off-guard,
naked and lost in the light that dazzled us,
suspended in a timeless time, almost unreal,
tasted of magic.

Tonight's sky is starry.
The moon and the boats reflect of the water.
There is an air of celebration, and fireworks
lighten up the sky.

I look for you among the stalls on the avenue,
hear you in the sweet music coming from afar.
It dissolves with the shouts of joy from the guys
sitting on the benches, hugging each other,
in love with love.

I picture you in the painting of a painter
sitting on the corner of the avenue, intent
to spy on the prying eyes of passers-by,
who pose indifferently to stare
at the eternal of a picture.

Everything looks as it did then.
Only time is no longer an ally,
witness of life and love,
which does not want to leave.

Rosy Gallace

So, I Looked at You

I looked at you for so long.
While absorbed, you thought
with your eyes closed.
So, I observed your wrinkles
– the expression of our time –

And the hunched shoulders
that in the brown wool sweater
mark the weight of your toil.

I looked at your gnarled hands,
trembling
but calm and welcoming,
still capable of consoling
and soothe the heart.

So, I saw you, you know,
sometimes afraid, like a robin
looking for food when autumn
gives way to the cold winter.

You looked beyond the horizon,
collected in the silence,
lifelong companions.

Destiny is now written,
and tomorrow the mists will come,
the wind will bring drops of frost,
good and evil won't make sense anymore.

We will be still here:
defying the wings of solitude,
holding on to the few vital sparks
stolen from the invisible thread of days,
intertwining our hands so as not to feel alone.

With the sails unfurled by the waves
we will let ourselves be rocked until
a drop of the nectar of love
makes sweet
our last winter.

Other Was that Time

We were born under different moons
between East and West
in a unique and unrepeatable
astral conjunction.

We were born from a rainbow
that arrived unexpectedly
without a thunderstorm
in the shades of colors,
in the autumn/winter equinox.

We are angels
who do not live in the same sky
but always together in the story.
Now and then, a new paragraph,
and everything starts again.

Meanwhile, grows this damned
and insolent nostalgia that takes
away the breath and sleep
on the hot nights of the city.

I don't ask you if you remember the summer of '70,
the processions of village feasts
or the evenings sitting on boats waiting for dawn
to trace again on the sand footprints
before the wave carried them away forever.

Other was that time!

And now, don't ask me to stay;
I no longer belong to the changing of your seasons.
You breathe the morning breeze
in the rustle of the sheets
between the warmth that is not mine.

Petals of Light

I stole from the wind
the sighs of blossoming
flowers for you.

I caught an eagle's flight
that smelled of rock
in the clear source of a limpid
and windy April morning.

I'll be a grain of wheat for you
that on the clods of my silence
will be reborn to be an ear.

I'll steal dust from the moon,
fragments from the stars
to illuminate your way.

With patience, I will weave
in your heart diadems of light
that you'll admire lightly,
like petals of roses
in the garden of your days.

I'll walk in the footsteps of your journey,
I will face your gaze,
proud and sincere, I will wait for you,
where the sun never sets,
and I will offer you a dawn
dressed only in hope.

In a Time to Come

On winter evenings
when you'll sing the lullaby,
you will recite the nursery rhymes,
you'll tuck a baby's blankets.
In that instant, I will be.

When you will accompany him
in his first uncertain steps,
and you'll read his first notes in the diary.

When you will seat around a large table
for the Christmas holidays
and you will taste kneaded sweets
with dried figs, walnuts, and chopped almonds.
That's when you'll remember me.

When in the evenings you'll wait behind a window
the late coming home of a boy.
In the bright red of the embers
of a lit fireplace,
in the toasted slices of bread
seasoned with good oil and the scent of oregano.
That's where you will find me.

I call to my mind your revisiting
the places of my childhood.
Between the lines of this yellowed sheet
that you just found behind that wardrobe
…..and then …
In every beat of your heart,
as often as you'll want,
in that time, I'll be.

Intertwining Souls

There was a scent in the air
of coming spring,
and I walked in the light breath of silence.

In the cool dew of a bright morning
I listened to the chirping of swallows; I saw
the cherry tree exploded into bloom,
primroses and violets,
the clothes hanging on the terrace
that talked about families
and of values upheld with tenacity.
Even the sky seemed to be dormant.
Everything smelled of eternity.

So, you arrived, in perfect silence
among the forsythia buds and all of a sudden
tasted of temporary,
of bitterness and helplessness.
I found myself infinitely small and fragile,
spying on pain on the edge of the sky.

Deserted streets, narrow alleys to border
the blue of the sky, shadows without faces, and a slow
life. An unreal silence between one night and the next,
filled with insomnia and thoughts while you travel
faster than light, without making a noise,
hungry for souls, asking for tears and no pity.

Now that the frost has touched the earth
and the colors are not of a rainbow,
even in pain I remain listening
in a suspended time, a loom of hands
that intertwine and pray within the soul.
I'll wait between bits of rosaries and words
until the life we want comes back
in the bright awakening of a new day.

(COVID-19)

Now That the Silence has Fallen Forever

Now that the silence has fallen forever
and the words have no longer a voice,
these days of clouds that cover the hours
in a day without light make no more sense.

Now that mistakes grow like woodworm
and consume our regrets, we still rest
to look at how colored a sunset is before
the darkness of a long night surprises us.

We have nothing left, just white ash in the
midst of fingers. We who chased time
between the songs of seasons on a seesaw,
running after us in the echo of daily lives.

Now that we have lost even the years among
the blades of grass of our twenties, among the
silences in the breath of thoughts, in the rustle
of words, I still find you in the glitter of the dew.

But now that time has submerged us
as it slipped on us in a flash, without
giving us the time to understand that now
we're different, and it's too late to sew the tears.

The film is over, and it is no longer necessary
to speak softly like the wind in April evenings.
In the end, we have lived this life side by side
between days of sun, fog, and pain, and that's it
what remains of us.

If You Were Here

I would not feel the unbridgeable void
in these long summer days.
I'd forgive even the chirping of cicadas
that took away the sleep from your nights.

I would run to you to find
the answers to my silences.
I would ask you how to live:
get up, get dressed, wash, eat,
keep that pain a secret,
the pain that takes the breath away.

I would fly to you on dark days;
I don't know where else to go.
I'd find relief among those walls
that smelled so much
of lavender and talcum powder.

If you were here
I wouldn't be so lost tonight,
confused and cold. I'd have a smile
and a warm hand, that word you
whispered in a low voice and how
magically everything turned as before.

This time I'd take you by the hand,
proudly I'd lead you along the course,
even on that chair you hated so much
but happy to show yourself with me.

I would touch a kiss on the folds
of the forehead while you travel in
your memories in a smile shielded
from a grimace of pain.

Lives in Parallel

The elapsed time will not be enough
to shorten distances, as won't be
enough a shy May sun to pick a ripe ear.

Lives that seek each other and
move away without a junction point.
They travel on fast trains, stopping
at the usual stations, never
meeting even for farewells.

They live time by leafing through calendars
with dates circled in red so as to remember.
They're shadows on the tracks that dissolve
in the evening between fireflies and moths.

They walk out of habit on
the usual roads by counting
the steps, not to forget.

They still toast on the night of the end of year
between the fireworks and the bubbles that
vanish in an instant, chasing
tomorrow in the sun of the afternoon, inside
the walls of a building that no longer exists.

The last winter will not be enough to resist
the gray days, boredom, and indifference.
It will not be enough to continue to believe
that love, friendship, art, and beauty improve
time without stealing words from the diary of heart.

Now, I'm no longer afraid, rather I'm surprised
to think that despite everything, I love our
wrinkles stuck on us, a mirror of our loneliness
that leads us to the surrender.
We are fully aware of our poor frailties.

What Remains of Us

The fullness of the best years
that time has stolen
remains of us.

Remain the processions in the squares,
the long hair of the children of flowers,
the flared trousers,
the dark cellars where hands touched
and gazes were cut
between the naivety of the red cheeks
in the dreams that were born.

The time between escapes and returns,
then the stops between tears and smiles.
Those dinners on summer evenings by
candlelight on the golden shores of the lake.
Dates marked in the diary of each year,
of lost birthdays and Christmas wishes.

Remain all those cold winter nights
that slipped slowly while waiting
near the house. Remains that secret
kept over time in a poignant, deep pain.
The regret confuses a blunder for love,
for not having known how to wait.

Remain the notes of songs to slow
the breath of an already tired heart
while life slowly escapes and moves away.

Remain the errors tattooed on the hands
between the folds of the years.
The roses found on the door when even
the last thorn becomes flattery.

Remain the memory that soothes and
intertwines nostalgia and the memories
of sunny days and lightning storms and
that red rose at least once without thorns.

Rosy Gallace

Traces

The stream flowed slowly over
a bed of time-honed stones
between the narrow banks of
moss, verbena, and cyclamen.

The games of children between
gushing flashes, races of tadpole
traps and grateful to croaking green,
triumph to whoever won the capture first.

The sky above the meadows was blue
and our hearts beat as we ran through
the vineyards to get drunk in the sun.
The wind chased us behind the shoots,
wittingly untying our braids
and playing ponytails
in the jump of the rope.

We then were caught by the sunset
in the alleys of the village, while the sun
drew shadows between the houses and at
the windows that opened to the street cool.

We waited for the night in the silences
of the squares and bell towers asleep
to collect fireflies of stars then
and close them for fun in a glass.

We have stolen caresses in the naive blush
of the cheeks and have woven wreaths
of dreams and hopes for a future
distant and unknown to us.

Traces of children were lost in these villages!

Stories that scratch the memory
and return as soft voices
to breathe distant nostalgia,
giving voice to the silence of time
for what we are now, dreaming
of caressing stars, exchanging them
for fireflies with no more glare.

A Day

I'll tell you about a day
when snow petals
whitened the lawn
as cotton candy.

When at the first smile of dawn
we got dressed in wind
getting up in flight among seagulls
springing free between sky and seas.

I'll tell you about ancient memories
flipping through crumpled notebooks
lulled by the notes of the old Banjo
played by your father.

I'll tell you about this day
sitting like time on smooth stones
at the edge of the river that, slow and sinuous,
runs along the shores.
Innocent playmate.

I'll caress your hands as lightly
as you touch the now out of tune strings
of your father's old Banjo
that still gives life to our days,
erasing our solitudes.

The Place of Silence

I haven't learned yet
to walk without shoes,
that noise that was already
a sign of life upon awakening.

I haven't learned yet to know
the silence of absence,
that door always closed
that I meet every morning,
waking up without the coffee
scent and that mess in the room.

If words weren't blades
and the red you see is only
the red of poppies.
If words had a heart
they would also have eyes
to look inside a pain.

If memories had a memory,
even the gestures of habit
would tell the days of that time
you embroidered on the canvas of a future.

It is a trunk, this body,
that meets its cracks and
hides the wounds in the hollows.

No shoes are needed,
nothing makes noise anymore.
Silence has taken its place in the rooms,
the wind blows hard to hear no longer
the echo of the words.

A Timeless Time

My time drags by
tearing days from calendars.
I write words you'll never read.

I walk through roads, narrow
streets and alleys, stumbling,
falling, repeating monologues.
Fragments of thoughts articulated
on the changing rhythms of breaths.

I have walked a thousand ways,
my burden of years and dreams
locked in memory to look for you
in the rising and the dying out,
in the reflection of the light
of days and nights,
in the alchemy of an image,
of a timeless time.

I find you in the cold air
of this morning, in the breath,
among whirlpools of smoke that
cloud the glasses, among laces and
patterns adorning tree branches.

Among the icy waters of the lake,
in shapeless designs, crystal garlands
on a muffled December day.

I would like to stop this time
in the skilled hands of a painter,
to find it, then in its immense beauty intact,
remained closed in the fragility of a soul
of this poem that came from the sky,
which makes us naked like branches of trees
                        swung by the wind.

Rosy Gallace

Some Days

There were certain days
on the shores of the lake
when glances were lost
in the golden sunsets
or in the shade of beech
and pine trees,
and naivety breathed
the age of modesty.

The tenderness of a hug
was hidden in the blond
of the brooms, inebriating
the memory with perfume,
since life was only real life,
crossing the border
between dream and reality.

And in the evening breeze,
the dim light on the tables
was barely enough to
read your last verses.

There are certain days
in sunny afternoons of silence
and on sleepless nights,
small flashes return
to where reality has
already crossed the border.

From the tight sieve of silences,
no more words filter out,
and the verses are
in a tired past.
The two of us
are now
voiceless silence.

The Last Season

I walked the seasons of the heart,
when a single glance was enough
to fill even the pockets with sunshine.

Hands intertwined and equal steps,
chasing dreams and happy evenings
around an ever-burning log.

I have run after time to grab
the moon with the fingers, when everything
seemed easy and possible with your steps beside.

Then the daring climbs turned fearful,
the legs no longer the same as before
and the seasons of lightning storms,
the fog to discolor the dreams,
the bitter cold inside the walls.

I've collected your senseless gestures,
and the long interminable silences
that took away the light from the days.

I filled vats of memory
that tasted of must and gall,
pressing time to grab
moments of solitude and love.

Now that the days are short
and my fingers reach the moon,
I no longer have your steps beside me,
silences are deafening thunder.

Yet, in those gestures, I still find
your fingers interwoven with mine
and the patience to stop time
in the last season of the two of us.

Rosy Gallace

May Days

Sit next to me,
I'll tell you
of that time of May.

They were long
and sunny days,
and we filled them
with joys and raids
flying in our lands,
fragrant with the aroma
of vine shoots.

While the grain grew
and the poppies red stood out
among the golden ears,
we hid ourselves
in the innocence of naivety.

Now that the time has stopped
and hours unfold in silence,
I watch the last rose of hedge,
freshly blossomed
in the season of the bride,
what you once offered to me
in a repeated gesture of love.

Like a heart that hopes and
awaits the autumn rain
coming down to nourish
the tender stem, I too in the
folds of wrinkled hands,
hold the last story of a life,
which, as a secret fairy tale,
give to you in these last days of May.

The Expired Time

It wasn't the highway kilometers
that made us feel distant.
It wasn't the labor
or the cost of the tolls.

It wasn't even
a round trip on an easy jet.
It was our thoughts
so distant… and… different.

Our time has traveled
between parallel lives
chasing each other, never meeting.

Our thoughts intertwined
with the days filled with loneliness;
now, they're here in their nakedness.

Our time has expired.

For once, without finding any holds,
let's look at each other through sincere
eyes and beyond words, let us listen
to the rhythms of heart, let's shake
hands, be real, let's just be ourselves.

Dreams Haven't Fallen

Only small noises
on a usual feast day.
A few sleepy hours
while forsythia stalks
raise to the sky the gems.

The ambitions, dreams,
or hopes haven't fallen,
not even the desire to
feel the excitement
of walking beside you
without hearing the
echo of my footsteps.

I won't give you sleepless
nights, I'll give you words.
They will cling to the walls
with footprints for you to hear
in the long days of autumns.

I'll hide in your silence
and will retrace the times when
everything seemed possible,
when the age ran more than us,
on blue days and clear nights,
in the innocence of my years
and the red dresses of poppies.

Now that I have reached time,
I slow my pace; I slide between
bites of sweetness, where dreams
and illusions remain intact,
imprisoned in blue paintings as
the world slowly moves away
between the depths of thought.

At the First Glare of Dawn

A strip of light
passes through the slits of shutters
as the first glow of dawn
reaches lightly
outlining your silhouette on the wall.

Your breathing is calm.
I can feel the beats between
the closed lashes of a child.
Wagner's music
blurs the loneliness
as you tie your necktie
looking in the mirror.

The remaining time is so short
that I can't wait any longer
in the melancholy of autumn.
I will open the door, as always,
I'll greet you; it will be the last.

The time has come to collect
the few days left. The branches
are naked, and I, a yellowed leaf,
will never let myself be trampled upon
by your silence, I won't wear smiles,
I will leave you my fragility, my insecurity.

I'll dress in light to brighten
my shadows, and if a trickle flows
down my face, I won't be afraid to show
myself crying lulled within tears of rain.

If even for a moment my heart stops,
I'll be reborn in the echoes of ancient memories.
Another sun will rise and warm that piece
of sky left in the shade in your absences.

I'll leave you these lines hanging on the branches,
taking away leaves to give them to the wind,
so you can no longer trample them
and confuse them with Wagner's music
at the first light of dawn.

The Unspoken Words

I have searched in the vocabulary of the mind
the right words to describe the days
when the sun did not rise in the morning
and the stars became stingy even in summer.

I have dug in the wrinkles of the hands,
rummaged through gray-mottled hair.
I've crossed so many burning deserts
looking through the grains of hot sand.

I have waited for the patience
digging knots in the trees
behind the winter flanks.

I have built a temple of memories
of my days, swallowing only
silences, expectations, regrets.

I've challenged life deceiving
time with my illusory dreams,
and you appear as an autumn mist.

And the reason falters.
The words searched over the years
are fragments shattered in an instant.
Everything appears in a fixed time
where my incompleteness crumbles.

The wind rises, and I'd like to scream
those searched and unspoken words,
for only one worthy of being shouted,
in a wall of pride remained closed.

Here it is, naked in my hands
the essence of life; breathe it
before the wind takes it away forever.
Call it love.

The Bill is Served

Scraps of paper
left here and there
in every corner of the house.

Pieces of life, of stories, of love
collected in one sentence
My love forever.

Fifteen years,
love in the chest, irrepressible
explodes in the air, in the skies,
crossing the cities.

A withered flower
between the pages of a book.

Wrinkly hands
barely raise it
my love, my life, the end.
Please, the bill is served
in the last piece of paper.

In the Folds of Time

The silence has returned to the rooms
on this last Sunday of summer,
already fragrant with autumn's perfume.

The suitcase on the door is full of seasons
and of numbers hanging on calendars.
All my words are beyond the weight,
so they remain mute at the bottom
of this day that is disappearing.

I know that your arms are not ready
to welcome today all my tears, so
you don't turn around to greet me.

I remain quiet, enclosed in the harsh
rustle of an engine that moves away,
before the night yields the last hour
to the day in the thought that flies over
the border, before space loses depth.

From the now tired branches, golden leaves
break free to follow you through your journey.
Each reaches you with a thought.

Meanwhile, I linger in the time folds
and drown in dishes full of emptiness,
of grudges, of words, so as not to feel
the distance in the days of absence.

Perhaps I will learn to understand
just in this not welcoming autumn
how much it costs us to remember,
not to kill a dream, or how to live
so as to give to this life meaning.

Your Restlessness

I'll clothe your ways with light,
and I will raise columns of joy
to drive away your melancholy.

With crystal fingers, I'll touch
all the strings of your heart,
and I'll awaken that emotion
waiting to strap on eagle wings.

I will drive away your fears
in the impenetrable spaces,
in the silence of labyrinths,
in the streets you can't find.

And I'll barter your fears
for the rest of my years
for that long-chased dream,
find answers you don't have.

If I could find in the fingers
the strength of the pen to write
in your day notebook, words
you'll read even without ink.

If in the skilled hands of an illusionist,
I'd entrust the fears of sleepless nights,
the anxieties, defeats, falls,
and as if by magic, see them disappear.

That embrace will be sweet
in the dawn of a new day, bright,
just like a rainbow after the storm.

I will raise my arms,
I will surrender unconditionally.

I'll travel in the few seasons to come,
I will slowly breathe my memories,
like the waft of wind in the desert,
and I'll stop where a trickle of rain
will still make sense.

The Silent Passage of Time

How can I explain to you
what the sound of your voice is like
when you ask me to hand you the glasses?

How can I tell you
what the taste of silence
interrupted by the rustle of newspaper pages feels like
as you sink into the news of the day?

Then I go back to sit in front of the window
with my book in hands
until the lines become invisible.

Slowly the lids droop
and drops of dew fall on the face;
I pick them up in my hands
as in a shell.

Then the verse lands on the sheet
and becomes an emotion. The breathing is light,
and the life in the chest hums like a stream.

Tranquil raindrops scratch the glass,
etching shapeless embroideries
in the evening that falls among the shadows
coming down from the sky with slight bows.

The night drags on, and I think about time
that flows over our lives silently
while you pass through my thoughts
interrupted by a light vigil
that, from time to time, closes the curtain of dreams.

Lost in the Fog of the North

The wind had calmed down that time too,
and the smell of linden trees covered the silences.
Thoughts still chrysalis awaited crimson skies.

The reeds moved the clouds,
and we traveled in the most innocent dreams
between ears of wheat
and the red cheeks of poppies.

That was our time,
a stirring of words and sounds, like lightning
before the thunder in the light that lived there.

The floral skirt, the heart out of the chest,
and you taking a flight
to explore new shores in boundless horizons.
We had the cosmos in our hands.

Then, that time,
the kites that flew lost their colors.
The stars crumbled
like slate dust in our hands.
Thus, we got lost in the mists of the North.

That was when we got old.
Now, memory also weighs
in this strange morning light.

About the Author

Rosy Gallace was born in Guardavalle in the province of Catanzaro in Calabria and lives in Rescaldina, Milan.

In the 1960s she moved with her family to Legnano, Milan, where she studied and worked. Since her youth, she cultivated a passion for writing poetry and stories. Beginning in 2011 she participated in national and international literary contests and won numerous prestigious awards, including the Culture Award in 2014. In the same year, she was evaluated by the Mayor of the city of Rescaldina, Professor Michele Cattaneo for her commitment to culture.

Her works have been included in several anthologies of contemporary poetry. Rosy Gallace is the creator, organizer, and president of several literary contests and poetry reading sessions along with book presentations. She also juries various literary competitions. Moreover, she is a singer in Rescaldina's Santa Cecilia Choir and voluntarily teaches the Italian language to foreigners.

She has published several books of poetry: "Small fragments," "Remaining days," "Unspoken words," and "Traces of memory." She has acted in the presentation of the theater opera, "Shadows of tormented memory," written and directed by the poet, writer, and producer Fabiano Braccini in memory of the victims in the Nazi concentration camps. She is also the production secretary of the theater. The play has been performed at various Italian theaters.

Her books have been translated into English, Romanian and Albanian by the translator, poet and writer Irma Kurti.

About the Translator

Irma Kurti is an Albanian poet, writer, lyricist, journalist, and translator and has been writing since she was a child. She is a naturalized Italian and lives in Bergamo, Italy. All her books are dedicated to the memory of her beloved parents, Hasan Kurti and Sherife Mezini, who have supported and encouraged every step of her literary path.

Kurti has also won numerous literary prizes and awards in Italy and Italian Switzerland. She was awarded the Universum Donna International Prize IX Edition 2013 for Literature and received a lifetime nomination as an Ambassador of Peace by the University of Peace, Italian Switzerland.

In 2020, she became the honorary president of WikiPoesia, the encyclopedia of poetry. In 2021, she was awarded the title of *Liria* (Freedom) by the Italian-Albanian community in Italy. She received the Leonardo da Vinci and Giacomo Leopardi prizes from the Chimera Arte Contemporanea Cultural Association of Lecce. The same association also honored her with the European Ambassador Award and named her the Best Poet of the Year in 2022.

Irma Kurti collaborates with various newspapers, magazines, and websites in Italian, Albanian, and English; she publishes interviews with various individuals in the international literary scene and translations of poetry from all over the world.

Irma Kurti has published 26 books in Albanian, 21 in Italian, 15 in English, and two in French. She has written approximately 150 lyrics for adults and children. She has also translated 15 books by different authors, and all of her own books into Italian and English.